Life-Ch

MW00988905

"Bradford, You're Fired!"

A Story of The Super-Self

William W. Woodbridge

**Executive
Books**

Life-Changing Classics, Volume VI
"Bradford, You're Fired!"

Published by
Executive Books
206 West Allen Street
Mechanicsburg, PA 17055
717-766-9499   800-233-2665
Fax: 717-766-6565
www.ExecutiveBooks.com

ISBN: 0-937539-79-1

Printed in the United States of America

TABLE OF CONTENTS

INTRODUCTION

Bradford represents all of us. He reminds us that our real work life begins when we realize we do not just work for a company—we work for ourselves. And until we learn to do our very best where we are at present, we can never really expect to achieve maximum success in any of our future endeavors.

Bradford, You're Fired is a story of the *Super*-self inside of every man and woman that can be harnessed for the purpose of accomplishing great things in life.

At first, it seemed like Bradford's life ended when he was fired by Mr. James T. Mather. But you will discover how Bradford's life actually began the day he began the job of boss to his Super-self.

This was his greatest turning point—the realization that his success began when he fired himself and said, "The next day I began the job of boss to my *Super*-self."

This timeless classic containing practical principles related to the importance of a positive work ethic and self-management skills will benefit any person who reads it.

"Bradford, You're Fired"

By William W. Woodbridge

"Bradford, you're fired!"

The door had opened silently behind me.

I turned from the cards that were spread on the table before me, and looked into the stern eyes of James T. Mather, sales-manager of the Continental Dry Goods Company.

"You don't mean—" I stammered.

"Exactly that, Bradford," answered my employer, closing the door behind him. "We're through with you, and there will be another man in your territory next week. I have written you time and time again, I have given you advice, I have tried to awaken some ambition in you—but to no avail. A man like you needs the feel of steel before he amounts to anything. So I'm giving it to you straight. You're fired, fired because you are not worth the expense money it takes to keep you in the territory. You'll leave your samples here at this hotel, and your successor will pick them up Monday. You will receive a check as soon as it can come from the home office, paying you in full to the first of next month. We're through with you for all time, Bradford! *You're a failure!"*

And he turned and left the room.

* * * * * * * * * *

I sat, looking dumbly at the cards spread out face up before me.

Mechanically I began counting off threes, placing a card here and there, as the game of solitaire demanded.

The midafternoon sun crept across the table, and its sheen glinted unpleasantly in my eyes.

I rose and drew down the shade.

The gloom that settled over the room seemed to steal its way into my soul.

Fired?

Well, that didn't matter much.

I had been fired before.

I had never claimed to be a success—that is, I had never boasted of it to myself.

And after all, what was the use?

I had my own little philosophy.

We live but once.

Why not get out of it all there is in life while we live it?

Thus I argued that fateful afternoon in March.

And this was the evolution of my philosophy:

Living but once, we must get all there is in life as we pass along.

All of what?

Pleasure!

And what is pleasure?

The having of a time, a big time! With a regular bunch of regular fellows.

Work?

Sure, for we must work to live, and must live to have our regular little old times.

Work—but not too hard, for why be a slave?

No man gets what he is worth— for the boss can't pay enough—can't afford it.

So work just enough to pay for what you do—or just enough to stimulate the chances for a raise.

But live—be no slave—live!

See life, for we pass this way but once.

When we die we are a long time dead.

So live the life while the living's good.

And this was my philosophy—and the philosophy of my kind.

I had a good time. I was popular.

My friends thought me a success— such a success as my philosophy breeds.

But the gloom of the room, this chill March afternoon, seemed to enter my soul.

I went over to my grip in the far corner of the room.

The half filled bottle there would give me courage to face another fight for a place.

Another job!

It would be hard sledding, finding a place.

My record was against me.

But then, I'd been fired before. I was rather clever at landing positions.

I laughed mirthlessly.

"Here's luck, Bradford," I said to myself, raising the bottle to my lips, "a better job and an easier one."

And with my bottle as companion, I returned to my game of solitaire, in the gloom-light of the room.

*   *   *   *   *   *   *   *   *   *

My thoughts were drab.

I had been expecting for some time to lose out on this job. The line was a hard one—too many trunks to pack, too many hick towns to make. But I had no idea that old Mather himself would drop in on me. Come right into my room without knocking! What right had he to do that, anyway? Suppose I *was* playing solitaire in the middle of the afternoon. Can't a man ever take a few minutes off, when he's been travelling all the night before on a road that has no Pullman service? Should a man let his boss kick

11

him around like an office boy?

So I took another drink to encourage my resentment against Mather and the Fates that had brought him spying on me while out on my route.

The Fates had always been against me. I'd never really had a fair show in life. I was a man of temperament. How could a hard money-making plug like Mather appreciate the finer feelings of a man like me? Mather was a self-made man, coarse of soul, selfish in all things, caring nothing for the men he ruled. He'd made good by *driving men*. That was his secret! Always driving us poor dogs of the road. What did he know of the "life"! A man without feeling, a self-made man.

And I took another drink.

Why, Mather was no gentleman! Imagine a man butting into your room without knocking. But then, he had none of the finer feelings. Why, his very education he'd picked up himself.

If he'd been to college as I had, he'd have known how to treat a fellow being, but then, what can you expect from a slave driver, who worked up from the packing rooms? Mather was a disgrace to his house. When he went out to dinner with his men, everybody in the dining room knew that he had never been raised to that kind of thing. They say his father was nothing but a day laborer. It was a good thing that I had quit a firm who hired such a man to handle the sales end. It was beneath a man of my breeding to be associated with such a concern. What would the frat boys have thought five years before, if they had known that I would ever have to look up to such a man as my superior?

And so I drained the last drop from the bottle.

I rose unsteadily from the table.

Drawing up the shade, I stood before the window and watched the red sun sink behind the foothills of a western mountain range.

A great wave of resentment swept over me.

And in my heart, I damned Jim Mather, the man who had kicked me down.

I hated him with a hatred that was more intense than any emotion that had ever before entered my life.

Jim Mather, the brute!

The sun flamed like a red flag of resentment before me, as I stood swaying drunkenly there by the window.

And his words, as he had stood behind me, were still ringing in my ears:

"Bradford, you're fired!"

*   *   *   *   *   *   *   *   *   *

For a long, long time I stood there.

I nursed my grudge.

Plans of revenge began forming in my mind.

If that man Mather insisted on queering my game, I'd kill the brute.

Kill him!

What had I ever done to *him*, anyway?,

He had always had it in for me, from the very start.

He knew that the territory he had given me was the worst in the country.

The man before me had given it up in disgust.

Maybe he thought I didn't know that.

Pretty smart little knocker, this Mather beast, but not smart enough for John Bradford.

I wondered why I had taken all he said so meekly.

Well, it wasn't too late now.

Mather was still in this hotel. I knew this, for there was no train out until midnight.

I'd go up and have a few words with this high-handed sales-manager of a tight-fisted clothing house.

I'd have the satisfaction of showing him that no man could rub it into Me, just because he had a better job than I.

And so I turned and stumbled across the room.

*   *   *   *   *   *   *   *   *   *

It was dark now.

I turned on the light, and went to the dresser, where my tie and collar had been discarded.

And, then a strange thing happened, born perhaps of the distorted imaginings of a drink-crazed mind.

Instead of the reflection of *one* man, I saw *two* there in the tall mirror before me, *two* men, images of myself, and each of them looked me in the face.

I stared amazed!

And as I looked, I saw one of the figures turn to

the other, and point his finger at the companion figure's face. Then I heard, as truly as I have ever heard anything, this strange incarnation of myself cry in a voice of force and conviction:

"Bradford, you're fired!"

"Fired?" whined the other, in a snivelling wail.

"Yes, fired! Get out of me! I'm through with you, now and forever. You're a failure, through and through. Go! You're my worst enemy. You're ruining my business, you're ruining my life. Bradford, you're fired!"

The reflection of the second figure faded from the glass. The remaining man turned and smiled into my eyes.

Then the room swam round.

I clutched at a nearby chair.

Darkness smashed in around me.

I felt myself falling, falling, falling.

And then—oblivion.

*   *   *   *   *   *   *   *   *   *

"Bradford, wake up!"

I turned restlessly on the hard floor of my room.

"Bradford, wake up!"

I opened my eyes and rose to a sitting posture. The dim light of early morning penetrated the drawn curtains. It was cold, and I was stiff and sore from my night's sleep on the thin carpet.

"Bradford, wake up!"

And it was then I realized that it was myself who spoke, my true self, commanding in spoken words.

I rose and walked unsteadily to the window.

The cards still lay scattered about on the table, as I had left them. The empty bottle lay on the foot of my unused bed.

I threw open the window and drank in deep draughts of the crisp morning air.

The clouds of the night before were driven from my brain.

Then I turned and again approached the mirror.

I stood and looked at my reflection in the glass. My hair was matted on my forehead, my cheek was smeared with grime from the carpet where I had lain, my eyes were red with the drink of the night before and my lips were dry and cracked.

I gazed at my reflection with a strange fascination. Could this be the culmination of twenty-eight years of developed manhood, this slinking, cowering figure of a bestial youth? And then I remembered the vision of the night before, and a strange conviction took possession of me, the conviction that the vision was a reality, that the night before I had actually seen what my befuddled memory now so persistently recalled to my drink-weary mind.

I leaned forward and peered into the eyes of my reflection—into the eyes of a man I hated and loathed, into the eyes of my one great enemy—John Bradford.

And then the great fight of my life began, the fight for possession of that which I had never before realized man possessed—the *Super*-self.

And to that cowering, slinking creature, that stood looking at me from the glass, I cried again:

"Bradford, you're fired! I'm going to put another man on your job, and the man on the job will be my slave, and I will be a slave driver, for it takes a slave driver to make a success. *Bradford, you're fired!* Get out of me, now and forever, for there's a new man to take your territory, and I'm going to see that the new man makes good. For I'm going to *drive* that new man to success, I'm going to hound him, day after day, every minute of every day. And I'm going to *own* this other man, instead of his owning me. I'm going to be his boss, Bradford, and he will respect me and do my bidding. You're a failure, Bradford. You had your chance, and you fell down. So you've got to go— forever, you and your philosophy with you. I'm through with you. *Bradford, you're fired!"*

But the face peered at me cynically from the glass. There seemed to be a sneer on his lips and the bloodshot eyes leered defiantly.

My nerves were drawn taut, and the blood burned hot in my veins.

I felt my head swim again, as the face in the glass mocked me.

"You can't fire me, you *can't* fire me, *you can't, you can't!"* the eyes seemed to say.

"Then I can kill you!" I cried, and turning to my bed, I took the empty bottle and flung it with all my strength at the tall mirror.

There was a crash and a rain of tinkling glass.

And that is how I "fired Bradford." Thus my real

fight for success began.

*　*　*　*　*　*　*　*　*　*

It was late in the afternoon when I descended to the lobby of the hotel.

Mather was sitting in the writing room.

"Mr. Mather," I said, as I stopped by the writing desk, "I want to have a talk with you."

"No use, Bradford."

"I know it, so far as the old job is concerned. But I want to get you to give me some advice. You see, I have taken on a pretty big contract this morning, and I thought maybe you might help me out."

He looked puzzled.

"Oh, very well," he said, folding up the papers before him and rising, "let's go out in the lobby, where we can talk unmolested."

"Mr. Mather," I began, when we were seated, "I have just been appointed sales-manager for a mighty big concern, and I have a salesman working for me who is a hard man to handle. I am not used to being boss, and this fellow is one that requires pretty strict curbing."

Mather looked at me in amazement.

"Say, Bradford, what is this, a joke?"

"I should say not, Mr. Mather, it's grim reality. This man has a hard job ahead of him. He's taking the place of a man who has the territory badly spoiled. The company had to fire the other fellow because he was a hard drinker, a gambler and a man who thought of but one thing, *cheap pleasure*. Now this new man who is to follow him has to remake the reputation of the house that the other fellow ruined. I think he's got good stuff in him. But he's got to be properly handled. He's the kind of a chap that needs a tight rein. I've faith in him, but he's going into a territory full of temptations and pitfalls, and I want to know what is the best way for me to help him make good for himself and for his house."

Mather seemed interested.

"Bradford, if I had a man of that kind working for me," he said, after a moment's reflection, "I'd start right off by gaining his entire confidence. I'd make him feel that the house was with him. I'd talk with him whenever I could, get him to believing that the success of the business depended on *his* efforts. And, Bradford—I'd give that man so much work to do that he would have no time to loaf on his job, no time to find temptations, and no time for temptations to find him. I'd *make* work for him—to keep him going hard. Then if there was anything in him, it would crop out."

"Thank you, Mr. Mather," I said, as I rose to leave him.

"But, Bradford," called Mather after me, "who is this man you are so interested in?"

"My Super-self," I answered, "and his job is the selling of Success, the Success of John Bradford."

Mather laughed unpleasantly.

"I might have known you were trying to string me," he said.

"Not a bit of it," I replied. "Just wait 'til I have made a success of this man that I have become the boss of. Then you will admit that I am in dead earnest. Mather, I am serious for the first time in ten years."

But Mather only laughed incredulously as I left.

*   *   *   *   *   *   *   *   *   *

"Bradford," I said to my *Super*-self, that night, "I'm going to talk this business over with you every day. I'm your boss now and I want you to know that

I have every confidence in you. It's a great thing to have the confidence of the boss. I'm going to be a hard boss, for I have your interest at heart. If you know this, and realize this, I believe you will succeed. After all, the success of any business depends on the boss and his relations with his employes. Am I right, John Bradford?"

And the John Bradford that looked at me from the mirror of my own room at home laughed confidently into my eyes.

"You see, Bradford, that last man I had working for me was a slacker—always afraid he'd do more than his bit. For a while, I thought I had a good man working for me. But he pretty near ruined the company, and the best piece of work I ever did was when I canned him. And it's the only thing to do, Old Man. Fire 'em bodily when they don't deliver the goods. You agree with me, don't you, Bradford?"

And this new John Bradford agreed with me perfectly.

"Now, old man, we've got a good line of stuff to sell, but a rotten reputation to live down. That means we will have to sell our goods pretty cheap for a while, until we show folks what we have. But if you have confidence in the house, and will buckle under the load that I'm going to pile on, we'll make a success of it, Bradford, you and I. Are you with me?"

And the eyes of my *Super*-self met mine squarely, and the battle was already half won.

*   *   *   *   *   *   *   *   *   *

The next day I began the job of boss to my *Super*-self.

"Bradford," I said to my *Super*-self, as we started out, *"success is a seed that can grow wherever it's planted;* what we're looking for is a place to *start sprouting.* Now go to it and win!"

And all day long, I drove my *Super*-Self from place to place, always seeking employment, always being turned down. The whole town seemed to know of the old Bradford, who had lost six positions in less than three years.

And so for a week, we plodded from office to office, always meeting with the same rebuffs, always refused consideration.

"Bradford," I said Saturday night, after that hardest of hard weeks, "I am proud of you. While you have not succeeded in making a sale, you have *succeeded in fighting off discouragement.* Your courage is still as high as it was when we began work. Your confidence in the house is still undimmed. Old boy, I know you will make good. Stick to it, and we're *bound to win!"*

And the assurance that shone in the eyes of my *Super*-self was the great joy that I carried into the next week.

* * * * * * * * * *

The Morton Drygoods Company was the largest wholesale concern in the city.

They travelled fourteen salesmen.

I had instructed my *Super*-self to call there first.

And Harry B. Wilson, the sales-manager, had refused to consider the application of John Bradford.

"Mr. Bradford," he had said, "we need no more salesmen at this time, and I feel that I should tell you frankly that even if we did have a vacancy, we would not care to entertain your application. You must realize, without my going into the matter further, why I could not give *you* any consideration."

After two weeks of unsuccessful endeavor, I had another long talk with my *Super*-self.

"Old man," I said, "there is something radically

wrong with us, and I am going to confess that it's largely the fault of the boss. You have been plugging along in great shape, doing just as I have instructed you to, but I failed you on your first call. No support from your sales-manager! We should have landed Morton. We'll go back there and *get that job.*"

"But how?" asked my *Super*-self.

"A salesman never sold goods to a new customer until he got him to look over the samples. We've got to spread out the goods for him to see, and land some kind of an order, even if it's a small one."

*   *   *   *   *   *   *   *   *   *

The next morning, I again called at the office of Mr. Wilson.

"Mr. Wilson," I began, "I made a great mistake when I called here last week."

"Yes?" queried he.

"Mr. Wilson, I am going to work for the Morton Drygoods Company, *regardless of salary, regardless of territory, regardless of the kind of work you put me to*. I want to convince you that I can make good. You have in your employ more than a hundred people, and there is certainly an opening some-where, in some department, some minor job——"

"Maybe," smiled Mr. Wilson, "you would like a job driving a dray? We're paying our draymen three dollars a day."

"When do I begin?" I asked. Mr. Wilson laughed outright. "You're joking."

"That's what every one seems to think about me. I am not joking! I want a job—quick—right away—now. Do I get it?"

Mr. Wilson looked at me for a moment in silence.

"Bradford," he said, bluntly, "You're a man with a bad reputation. While I never knew you personally before you came into the office last week, I've heard of you frequently. Your record is against you. It would be folly for you to try anything spectacular here. If you drove a dray, you would be a drayman and nothing else, with no hope of advancement and no help from me whatsoever. I do not want a man with a reputation like yours on my sales force! There are too many good men wanting jobs without gambling on recognized failures like yourself. With that understanding, of course, I can probably get you in as a laborer."

That night, as I unfolded a package containing a new suit of overalls, I said to my *Super*-self:

"After all, it may look like a small order, but it's a poor salesman who does not book an order because it's too small. *We've planted the seed.* Now, it's up to you to make it grow. *We'll pick success from that bush yet,* if a hard task master can keep you working. Are you with me?"

And my *Super*-self was true to his promise of the past.

* * * * * * * * * *

Six months passed.

I was a hard boss!

My *Super*-self was on the job always, a few moments before any of the rest of the crew.

He was the last to leave.

He kept his horses, his harness, his dray, in the prime of condition.

28

He took pride in his work.

He was a drayman.

Not much to be proud of?

It was his *work,* his *livlihood,* his *life!*

And I was proud of my *Super*-self.

*   *   *   *   *   *   *   *   *   *

Mather passed me on the street one day, as I was unloading packing cases onto the sidewalk.

"Bradford!" he exclaimed. "Isn't this quite a comedown from sales-manager for a great concern?"

"Comedown? I should say not! I'm still sales-manager, Mr. Mather, and I'm making good!"

Mather laughed and passed by.

A few weeks later, Wilson sent for me.

"I want you to tell me," he said, "just why you are a failure instead of a success. I'll admit I have been watching you at your work, for a man of your standing is a novelty as a drayman. Bradford, you have made a good drayman. I congratulate you. Tell me, why did you make such a mess of it as a travelling salesman?"

"John Bradford failed as a salesman," I answered, "because he had the wrong kind of a boss; he worked *for* a concern, not *with it*. He believed that he was giving more than he got. He lived for what he could *get* out of life, not what life would *give* him. John Bradford was a failure because his definition of success was wrong. John Bradford was a drunkard and a slacker. That's why I fired him."

"Why you fired him!" exclaimed Mr. Wilson.

"Exactly. I fired John Bradford! Literally kicked him out of my life. Then I became the boss of a new man, a clean man, a man who was interested in *me*. I became *his* boss, his sales-manager, and he's worked for me ever since. No man is a success unless he has authority over something—and I now have authority over myself, my *Super*-self. And so I have already succeeded—and this success must bear fruit in time. *I have the patience to wait."*

"You are surely not expecting me to believe this?"

"Mr. Wilson, I realized that the old John Bradford was a failure. Mather, of the Continental, discovered it before I did. He fired John Bradford. I realized that if John Bradford was not good enough man for the Continental he was *not good enough for me!* So I fired him too. I found and set to work a *better* man, a man in whom I could place every confidence. That is man's first duty. The man who works for me now I *believe in.* He is a success. It may take years for the world to find it out; but it must in time, and so I am driving my *Super*-self, day after day, doing what there is to do as well as it is within our power to do it. Untiring energy, ambition, confidence, and a clean heart will win for any man! This I require of my *Super*-self!"

The next day, I was offered a try-out with the Morton Drygoods Company, in the old territory where I had failed.

My *Super*-self worked manfully, and *succeeded.* It was hard work, but my *Super*-self had been trained by this time to *love hard work.* My old trade did not welcome me back into the field with any enthusiam, but my *Super*-self and I made enthusiasm for ourselves. And orders began coming into house regularly.

A raise in salary followed the first trip over the territory.

And so for two years I covered the field, and never once did my *Super*-self fail me.

And then came the proudest day of my life.

For it was then I received a letter from Robert G. Marshall, president of the Continental Drygoods Company, Inc., asking for an interview.

"Mr. Bradford," began Mr. Marshall, when I was seated in his private office, "I understand that you once were in our employ."

"Some years ago," I replied.

"There seems to have been some very unfortunate mistake made, Mr. Bradford. Our records show that you were let out by our sales-manager, Mr. Mather."

"Yes," I replied, "Mr. Mather fired me."

"Very unfortunate, Mr. Bradford, very."

A silence for a moment, then—

"The territory you covered for us brought in very good business for about a year after you left it, but when you returned into that field for the Morton people, our business began to suffer. Would it be asking too much of you to tell me how much *your* sales from that territory amounted to this last season?"

I mentioned the amount.

"Mr. Bradford, I will be equally frank, and tell you that no two of our men sent in as much as that last season."

Again the silence.

I feel that I am not acting unethically, Mr. Bradford, in making you the offer that I am about to make, in view of the fact that you are really an old Continental man. We want you to come back with us. I sometimes think that perhaps Mr. Mather is not quite the man to handle our sales end, and I am wondering if you would care to consider taking the position of sales-manager for us."

"Mr. Marshall," I replied, "you are doing my good friend Mather a great injustice. My success in life is due altogether to the following of Mather's advice and example. The best thing he could have done for you was to have fired John Bradford. In fact, I thought so well of it, that I did the same thing. I fired him myself."

"Bradford, You're Fired!"

"What's that? You fired John Bradford? Fired yourself?"

"Yes, Mr. Marshall, I did just that," I answered. "And, as to accepting your offer, this I regret is impossible, as I have just accepted the position of sales-manager of the Morton Drygoods Company. I feel that I owe them too much to leave them now."

And so James T. Mather is still sales-manager of the Continental, and I am still *boss*—Boss of my *Super*-self!

And in this story of my rise, you may find the *secret of success*. If you have not succeeded, it is your own fault. First, realize that there is no success in life for you unless you are Boss. Be a *Boss*, a Man in Authority! Fire John Bradford, and put your *Super*-self to work! Make your *Super*-self serve you—and Success is already within your reach. And when doubts and fears assail you, remember the weaker man is no longer on your force. You are the boss of your self, of the *Super*-self, the inner man who waits to serve you. And what success has come to me in life is due alone to this talisman:

"Bradford, you're fired!"

*   *   *   *   *   *   *   *   *   *

ABOUT WILLIAM W. WOODBRIDGE

William Witherspoon Woodbridge, the author of *Bradford, You're Fired!*, was the gifted writer of a series of small booklets that revolutionized the lives of countless individuals in the early 1900s. And his compelling stories are still having a tremendous impact in our day and time.

Woodbridge is also the author of *That Something*, *Something More*, and *Scooting Skyward*.

That Something, a book that was a means of bringing success and "performing miracles" in the lives of many men and women, was one of his most popular titles.

William Woodbridge's life-changing short stories gained widespread recognition from many of the prominent leaders and dignitaries of his time. Thomas Edison remarked, "I have read *That Something*. It tells the whole story." And Emerson Harrington said, "It is a message that ought to go out to all men everywhere."

Stories like *Bradford, You're Fired*, along with other titles by Woodbridge, were popular for containing timeless wisdom related to principles of patience, hard work, integrity, and commitment.

Paul J. Meyer, the author and pioneer of the self-improvement industry whose programs have sold more than 2 billion dollars worldwide, attributes much of his success to his ability to harness William Woodbridge's *That Something* and make it work for him.

LIFE-CHANGING CLASSIC SERIES

COMING SOON

Seven Golden Rules of Milton Hershey

The Thirteen Success Principles of Ben Franklin

Andrew Carnegie and the Advantages of Poverty

The Price of Leadership by Charles "T" Jones

Sizzle Our Way Through Life The Wheeler Way by Dr. Ben Kain

WHAT IS A SALESMAN?

SOMEWHERE between the dollars that go into the pay-check (of every office boy, order clerk, stenographer, bookkeeper, office manager, purchasing agent, punchpress operator, printer, shipping clerk, foreman, plant superintendent, promotion manager, sales manager, vice president, president, and all the straw bosses) and the raw materials that start the long chain reaction that puts money in the till, there is the salesman.

Salesmen come in assorted sizes, shapes and colors, but they all have the same creed: To get as much as they can for as little as they can put out because the company is underpaying them anyway and making an absolute fortune off of them . . . what the company doesn't steal from them, "Uncle" takes in taxes.

Of all the optimists this side of Heaven, the salesman is the most. He hits on the first call and goes into orbit. His super-charger kicks in, and he knocks off three more sales before lunch. Two boosters at lunch cause a change of his course and re-entry into earth's atmosphere. A failure on the first call of the afternoon shuts off his super-charger and the friction of the second call burns up all his fuel. He decides he has had it and returns to home base. Optimists? You bet all salesmen are optimists. This is to them what fuel is for space ships.

He is the spark that ignites the fire. He is to business what fuel is to machinery. He is the indispensable man–But never let him know it. There is no hat large enough for an ego-inflated salesman. There is no club car sound proof enough for this ego-maniac. The front office, the back office, the in-between office are all fair game for this power-drunk, sales-contest winner with a full head of steam (and more than likely a full tank of fuel)—But God bless all of them—Their brass breaks the frost off the most frigid purchasing office and melts the heart of resistance to purchase. They have an unique kind of courage that is just as important in its contribution to the greatness of America as the courage of our most decorated G.I. or our bravest General.

PERSONAL DEVELOPMENT CLASSICS

We Are The Beloved	Blanchard
You and Your Network	Smith
The Common Denominator of Success	Gray
The Power of Positive Thinking	Peale
How to Win Friends and Influence People	Carnegie
Think and Grow Rich	Hill
I Dare You	Danforth
The Go-Getter	Kyne
How I Raised Myself From Failure to Success	Bettger
The Greatest Salesman in the World	Mandino
Move Ahead With Possibility Thinking	Schuler
Life is Tremendous	Jones
See You at the Top	Ziglar
The Success System That Never Fails	Stone
The Secret of Success	Allen
The Richest Man in Babylon	Clason
The Ultimate Gift	Stovall
The Traveler's Gift	Andrews
Freedom From Fear	Matteson
How to Win Over Worry	Haggai